RUNE STONES
UNLEASHING THE MAGIC WITHIN
By

J. Brownbridge

INTRODUCTION

Welcome to the enchanting world of rune stones, where ancient symbols hold the key to unlocking your inner power and manifesting your deepest desires. In this book, we embark on a transformative journey through the mystical realm of runes. Each page is dedicated to a specific rune stone, revealing its meaning, and providing guidance on how to harness its magical energy to manifest your intentions. So, open your heart and mind as we embark on this extraordinary adventure of self-discovery and manifestation.

Ansuz

Meaning: Communication, Divine Inspiration.

Symbol Placement: Draw the Ansuz symbol on the back of your non-dominant hand to enhance communication and inspiration and to invite spiritual growth and balance into your life. Visualize it as a conduit for divine wisdom and guidance.

Manifestation Technique: Meditate with the Ansuz rune stone, visualizing clear and effective communication in your relationships and endeavors. Carry the stone with you during important conversations or creative pursuits to enhance your ability to express yourself.

Berkanan

Meaning: Growth, Nurturing

Symbol Placement: Draw the Berkanan symbol on your lower abdomen to channel the energy of new beginnings and fertility. Focus on nurturing growth and manifesting your desired outcomes.

Manifestation Technique: Hold the Berkanan rune stone in your hands and visualize the aspects of your life where you seek growth and renewal. Create a nurturing space, surround yourself with natural elements, and affirm your commitment to personal transformation as you work with the stone.

Dagaz

Meaning: Enlightenment, Transformation Symbol

Symbol Placement: Draw the Dagaz symbol on your forehead, between your eyebrows.

Manifestation Technique: Place the Dagaz rune stone on your third eye chakra during meditation, focusing on your desire for enlightenment and inner transformation. Visualize the illumination of your path and the shedding of old patterns, allowing the stone's energy to guide you towards a higher state of consciousness.

Ehwaz

Meaning: Partnership, Fluidity

Symbol Placement: Draw the Ehwaz symbol on the inside of your wrist, near the pulse point.

Manifestation Technique: Hold the Ehwaz rune stone and visualize a harmonious flow of energy surrounding you. Imagine yourself effortlessly moving in sync with the rhythm of life, experiencing positive partnerships and fluidity in all areas. Affirm your intention for cooperative and supportive relationships. Carry the Ehwaz rune stone as a reminder to embrace partnership and remain open to life's flow.

Fehu

Meaning: money, abundance, luck

Symbol Placement: Draw the Fehu symbol on the palm of your dominant hand.

Manifestation Technique: Hold the Fehu rune stone in your hand and envision a life of financial abundance and prosperity. Carry the stone in your wallet or purse as a symbol of attracting wealth. Meditate on gratitude and take inspired actions to manifest your desired financial goals.

Gebo

Meaning: Partnership, Generosity

Symbol Placement: Draw the Gebo symbol on the inside of your wrist.

Manifestation Technique: Hold the Gebo rune stone and visualize harmonious partnerships and balanced exchanges in your life. Use the stone to infuse your relationships with love, kindness, and generosity. Wear it as a reminder to cultivate a spirit of giving and receiving in all your interactions.

Hagalaz

Meaning: Transformation, Challenges

Symbol Placement: Draw the Hagalaz symbol on the back of your non-dominant hand.

Manifestation Technique: Hold the Hagalaz rune stone and visualize yourself standing strong amidst challenges. Embrace the transformative power of difficulties and affirm your intention to grow and overcome. Carry the Hagalaz rune stone as a reminder of your resilience and the potential for positive transformation.

Isa

Meaning: Stillness, Self-Control

Symbol Placement: Draw the Isa symbol on the centre of your palm.

Manifestation Technique: Meditate with the Isa rune stone, seeking inner stillness and self-control. Find a quiet space, hold the stone in your hand, and close your eyes. Breathe deeply, letting go of distractions. Visualize a serene winter landscape, feeling the calmness and tranquility. Focus on cultivating self-control and clarity. Carry the Isa rune stone as a reminder to embrace stillness and exercise self-control in your daily life..

Jera

Meaning: Harvest, Patience

Symbol Placement: Draw the Jera symbol on the back of your non-dominant hand.

Manifestation Technique: Hold the Jera rune stone and connect with the cycles of nature. Visualize the fruition of your goals and practice patience as you await the harvest. Carry the stone with you as a reminder to stay grounded and aligned with the natural flow of time and manifestation.

Kenaz

Meaning: Creativity, Transformation

Symbol Placement: Draw the Kenaz symbol on the centre of your chest, over your heart.

Manifestation Technique: Meditate with the Kenaz rune stone, focusing on unlocking your creative potential and igniting the fire of transformation within you. Carry the stone with you during artistic endeavours or when seeking to bring about positive change. Allow its energy to inspire you and fuel your passion.

Laguz

Meaning: Flow, Intuition

Symbol Placement: Draw the Laguz symbol on the inside of your wrist, near the pulse point.

Manifestation Technique: Hold the Laguz rune stone and envision a gentle flowing stream of water. Connect with its energy and affirm your intention to trust your intuition and go with the flow of life. Carry the Laguz rune stone as a reminder to embrace intuitive insights and allow them to guide you towards greater harmony and fulfillment.

Mannaz

Meaning: Self, Connection

Symbol Placement: Draw the Mannaz symbol on the center of your forehead, between your eyebrows.

Manifestation Technique: Meditate with the Mannaz rune stone, focusing on self-awareness and connection with others. Find a quiet space, close your eyes, and breathe deeply. Visualize a golden thread connecting you to all beings, fostering empathy and understanding. Affirm your intention to embrace your authentic self and cultivate meaningful connections. Carry the Mannaz rune stone as a reminder of your interconnectedness and the importance of self-acceptance and compassion.

Naudiz

Meaning: Need, Hardship

Symbol Placement: Draw the Naudiz symbol on the back of your non-dominant hand.

Manifestation Technique: Hold the Naudiz rune stone and focus on building endurance and overcoming challenges. Visualize yourself standing strong and resilient in difficult times. Affirm your intention to thrive in the face of hardship. Carry the Naudiz rune stone as a reminder of your inner strength and your ability to navigate any obstacle. Embrace the lessons that come with hardships and trust in your resilience to endure and survive.

Othala

Meaning: Ancestral Wisdom, Heritage

Symbol Placement: Draw the Othala symbol on the inside of your forearm.

Manifestation Technique: Hold the Othala rune stone and connect with the wisdom of your ancestors. Visualize a deep connection to your heritage and the guidance it provides. Use the stone as a conduit to tap into ancestral knowledge and honor your lineage. Keep it nearby during rituals or when seeking guidance from your ancestral spirits.

Perthro

Meaning: Mystery, Divination

Symbol Placement: Draw the Perthro symbol on the center of your forehead.

Manifestation Technique: Meditate with the Perthro rune stone, inviting its energy to deepen your intuition and unlock the secrets of the unseen. Use the stone during divination practices such as tarot reading or scrying to enhance your connection to the mystical realms. Allow the stone to guide you in uncovering hidden truths and unraveling the mysteries of life.

Raidho

Meaning: Travel, Journey

Symbol Placement: Draw the Raidho symbol on the sole of your foot.

Manifestation Technique: Place the Raidho rune stone near your travel documents or carry it with you when embarking on a journey. Visualize safe and transformative travels, opening yourself to new experiences and personal growth. The stone serves as a talisman for protection and guidance during your adventures.

Sowilo

Meaning: Success, Vitality

Symbol Placement: Draw the Sowilo symbol on the crown of your head.

Manifestation Technique: Hold the Sowilo rune stone and visualize yourself radiating with success, vitality, and divine energy. Allow the stone's power to illuminate your path, inspire confidence, and propel you toward achievement. Carry it with you as a symbol of personal empowerment and a reminder of your limitless potential.

Teiwaz

Meaning: Protection, Strength

Symbol Placement: Draw the Teiwaz symbol on the back of your dominant hand.

Manifestation Technique: Hold the Teiwaz rune stone and visualize a shield of protective energy surrounding you. Use the stone as a focal point during rituals or meditation to enhance your inner strength and ward off negativity. Carry it with you to promote a sense of personal security and resilience.

Uruz

Meaning: Power, Endurance

Symbol Placement: Draw the Uruz symbol on the back of your dominant hand.

Manifestation Technique: Hold the Uruz rune stone and visualize yourself embodying strength and endurance. Connect with its powerful energy and affirm your intention to embrace your inner power. Carry the Uruz rune stone as a reminder of your resilience and ability to overcome challenges. Let its energy empower you to persevere and achieve your goals with unwavering determination.

Wunjo

Meaning: Joy, Harmony

Symbol Placement: Draw the Wunjo symbol on your solar plexus, just below your ribcage.

Manifestation Technique: Meditate with the Wunjo rune stone, cultivating feelings of joy, happiness, and inner harmony. Use the stone to shift your focus to the positive aspects of life and invite more joy into your experiences. Carry it with you as a talisman of happiness, spreading its uplifting energy wherever you go.

Algiz

Meaning: Protection, Courage

Symbol Placement: Draw the Algiz symbol on the inside of your forearm, near your elbow.

Manifestation Technique: Hold the Algiz rune stone and visualize a shield of protective energy surrounding you. Connect with its power and affirm your intention to embrace courage and seek divine protection. Carry the Algiz rune stone as a symbol of your inner strength and a reminder to trust in your ability to overcome obstacles. Let its energy instill you with a sense of bravery and provide a shield of divine protection in your life.

Eihwaz

Meaning: Stability, Resilience

Symbol Placement: Draw the Eihwaz symbol on the inside of your wrist, near the pulse point.

Manifestation Technique: Hold the Eihwaz rune stone and envision a tall and sturdy yew tree, symbolizing stability and resilience. Connect with its energy and affirm your intention to cultivate stability in your life. Carry the Eihwaz rune stone as a reminder to stay grounded and resilient in the face of challenges. Let its energy support you in maintaining a strong foundation and navigating life's ups and downs with grace and strength.

Thurisaz

Meaning: Protection, Transformation

Symbol Placement: Draw the Thurisaz symbol on the inside of your palm, near the base of your thumb.

Manifestation Technique: Hold the Thurisaz rune stone and visualize a powerful and protective energy surrounding you. Connect with its transformative energy and affirm your intention to embrace positive change and personal growth. Carry the Thurisaz rune stone as a reminder of your inner strength and the ability to overcome obstacles. Let its energy guide you in transforming challenges into opportunities for growth and protection.

Ingwaz

Meaning: Unity, Harmony

Symbol Placement: Draw the Ingwaz symbol on the center of your chest, over your heart.

Manifestation Technique: Hold the Ingwaz rune stone and visualize a harmonious and united energy flowing through your being. Connect with its power and affirm your intention to foster unity and harmony in your relationships and surroundings. Carry the Ingwaz rune stone as a reminder of your interconnectedness and the importance of cultivating harmonious connections with others. Let its energy guide you in creating a sense of unity and cooperation in your life.

Printed in Great Britain
by Amazon